Emotional Intelligence

For Living a Better Life, Becoming Successful at Work, and Experiencing Happier Relationships. Learn and Improve Emotional Agility, Your Social Skills and Discover Why it Matters More Than IQ

Alex Door

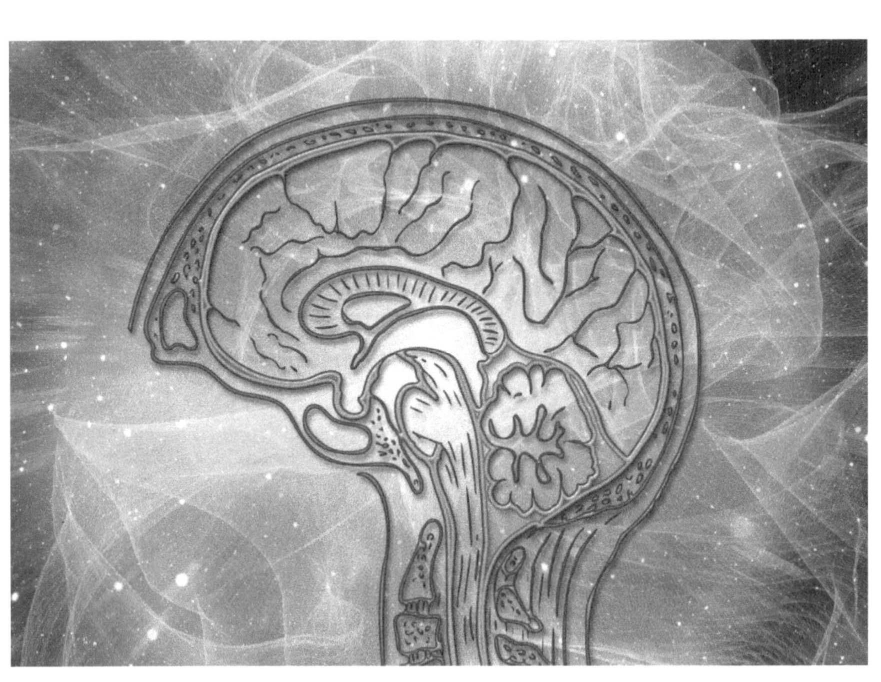

Table Of Contents

Introduction

Congratulations on purchasing *Emotional Intelligence: For Living a Better Life, Becoming More Successful at Work, and Experiencing Happier Relationships. Learn and Improve Emotional Agility, Your Social Skills and discover Why it Matters More Than IQ* and thank you for doing so. Every one of us has a variety of emotions that come out at different points in our day. They are often the result of external forces from our environment, but can also be affected by our own internal thoughts. Throughout the day, we have a number of thoughts and feelings that enter our minds, and we can do very little to control their influx. While the emotions we go through are a natural occurrence, we can certainly manage our emotions and use them to our advantage. When we talk about managing our own and other peoples' emotions, we are getting into the art of emotional intelligence.

The following chapters will discuss what emotional intelligence is, and how it is one of the most important skills to master for our professional lives, personal lives, health, and relationships. No matter where we are, we have emotions we need to deal with. It makes sense then that these emotions will impact our lives either positively or negatively, depending on how we react to them. In order to succeed in any area of our lives, we must be able to manage ourselves and our environment. This means that we cannot just learn to control our own emotions, but also the emotions of other people. When we have the ability to do this, we can accomplish great things. No matter how unbalanced the world around us becomes, when we are in control of ourselves, we are in control of our results. This may be easier said than done, but once we master the art of emotional intelligence, we will be able to control our destiny, manage our relationships positively, create much more opportunity for success, and just live a better life in general.

As the title suggests, we will examine many aspects of emotional intelligence and discuss why it is even more important than your intelligence quotient, or IQ. A common theme throughout this book will be the concept of emotional agility because it plays a big role in having emotional intelligence. Unfortunately, we will not always be able to manage our emotions in a calm and controlled environment. We will have to learn to be flexible with our thoughts and feelings in an everchanging world and must be able to use our emotions to respond to any situation we are faced with. The old saying that we can't control what happens to us, but we can control how we react is emphasized heavily within the subject of emotional intelligence. Our thoughts truly make up our actions, which make up our results. We will help you get great results through the art of emotional intelligence.

There are plenty of books on this subject on the market, thanks again for choosing this one! We not only want to explain in-depth the idea of emotional intelligence, but also illustrate how it can be utilized in our everyday lives no matter where we are or where we came from. Every effort was made to ensure it is full of as much useful information as possible; please enjoy!

Chapter 1: What is an Emotion?

Imagine receiving a phone call one day, and the person on the other end gives you some heartbreaking news. The news can be a number of things. What happens to us at this moment? We become saddened and can even become an emotional wreck. This is our natural instinct and there is nothing we can do to control the emotion. When we receive devastating news, we feel it in our core and the feeling of sadness oozes out of us. We cannot stop it. It will happen, even if it is just for a moment. This is true of any other emotion as well. When we receive good news, we become joyful and happy. When someone does something we dislike, we feel a wave of sudden anger. When we are in an unsafe situation, we get a sense of fear. These emotions are going through us constantly throughout the day, and day after day as we are moving about with our lives and being faced with many different circumstances. No matter how much we plan out our day, we will be faced with unknown and unforeseen situations. As a result, we will be overcome with massive amounts of feelings that will alter our mindset constantly.

What exactly is an emotion? Simply, it is defined as an instinctive or intuitive feeling or mood that is derived from our environment, people, circumstances, or our inner thoughts. There is really no consensus on what the definition of emotion should be; however, most people agree that it is inherent and cannot necessarily be stopped. We begin experiencing emotions immediately after we are born. Babies will instinctively cry, laugh, smile, moan or show any number of different acts related to their emotions. At what point we actually start understanding our emotions is anyone's guess. However, the fact that we are going through them from birth without having any knowledge shows that they are completely ingrained in us. While we are young and can't comprehend what is happening, our emotions will take over us constantly. Children usually react immediately to any type of stimuli and their feelings run wild. As we grow older and have the ability to assess what is happening, we have the ability to influence how we react.

Certainly, we have heard the terms controlling our emotions, suppressing our emotions, hiding our emotions, or letting our emotions out. We don't usually hear people say stop our emotions. This is actually impossible because, as we mentioned before, they are a part of us. While it is true that we cannot stop ourselves from feeling a certain way, we can guide these feelings consciously through learned behaviors and use them to our advantage. Yes, we can learn to guide our emotions through practice. We will get more in-depth on this topic when we start discussing emotional intelligence. For now, we will set the foundation further for what emotions really are.

Why are emotions so important? Why do we pay them so much mind? The fact is, emotions control our thoughts, and our thoughts control our actions, which will ultimately control our results. When we look at certain situations in our lives, like the people we keep, the job we have, the city we live in or the food we eat, we can really trace all of it back to our emotions. Let's look at this as an example: When you are in a very crowded area, you feel overwhelmed. This feeling of being overwhelmed leads to tremendous anxiety. As a result, you want to isolate yourself as much as possible. This causes you to stay indoors and avoid human contact altogether. While being in a secluded area for a day or two may not mean anything, being isolated for a long period of time can lead to other emotional issues. The dislike of being in a crowd can lead to feelings of isolation, depression, and sadness if it continues for too long. It can really become a vicious cycle.

Another example is the classic road rage incident. We may be using this quite often throughout this book. When you are driving on the road, and someone cuts you off or makes some other error, you instantly become upset and even angry. These feelings of anger may lead to you having thoughts of doing physical harm, which in turn, may cause you to react in a dangerous manner. This can result in a major road rage incident. You are not only putting your own safety in danger, but also the safety of everyone else that is near you. Allowing your emotions to take over you like this can not only be bad, but fatal. When we listen to the news, it seems there is a new story every few minutes of someone doing something ridiculous. What makes it even more interesting is why they did it. There are stories out there of people losing control at a restaurant because their food order was messed up. This does not seem like a situation that would cause someone to start acting erratically. However, some people do and it's because they cannot control their emotions. Truth be told, most situations out there would not warrant this type of behavior. In the end, it can all be chalked up to losing our minds.

As we can see, emotions are not something to take lightly. They affect every part of our lives, and if we let them get out of hand, our lives can be damaged in severe ways. The damage can become irreversible when actions are taken to the extreme. Imagine if the road rage incident turned into a fatal accident, all because one person could not handle becoming angry. How many lives could have been ruined at that moment? Think about all of the times people did something awful, maybe even unforgivable. In most, if not all, cases, they were simply reacting to their emotions in that current situation. If we allow our emotions to overtake us, they will. If we harness and control them, we can use them to our advantage in so many ways. What would be a good use of that anger that we feel on the road? We could take some deep breaths, or when we are able to get off the road, we could get a good workout in. These are just examples. Do not lose it on the road and cause havoc for no reason. The reactions we have to our emotions may not even have a major effect at that moment, but over time, they will have a cumulative impact on our lives. This goes for every emotion we have. In the next section, we will break down the various emotions and detail on how they impact our lives. There really are healthy and unhealthy emotions. However, if we are able to control and use any of them to our advantage throughout over lives, we will be successful.

Different Emotions Affecting Us

When we speak of emotions, we are speaking about a wide array of moods and feelings that we go through. We often experience these various emotions multiple times throughout the day, and sometimes even multiple times within a couple of minutes of each other. It may be fair to say that we can feel them at the same time. This truly puts us on an emotional roller coaster, as the saying goes. Let's discuss the major emotions that we go through on a regular basis and some of the issues that cause them.

Happiness

Out of all of the emotions, happiness is the one that people strive for the most. This is certainly no surprise. People want to be happy. They always want to be in a good mood. Whether they are able to achieve it or not is a different story. Happiness is characterized by joy, satisfaction and a state of well-being. It is defined as a pleasant emotion and through much research, it has been linked to increased longevity in life and increased satisfaction in a person's professional and personal life. Truly, being happy is a goal people strive for, but do not always obtain. It is impossible to be happy all of the time, but we can make it a regular emotion for us.

How does one obtain happiness? This is a very difficult question to answer because it really depends on the individual. What makes one person happy may mean nothing to someone else. In our society, happiness is often looked at from a more superficial and materialistic standpoint. Many people believe that if they have enough money, the latest gadgets, or the right job, they will be happy. Also, people believe that if they just get through a certain portion of their lives and reach their goal destination, they will also become happy. While these things can certainly contribute to our mood and our feelings, it is really much deeper than this. Happiness really comes with being in a place you want to be in life. What that means to you is very personal. Being happy is not a destination, but a way of life. Also, happiness is not simply a choice. This is a myth that has run amuck in our society. You simply cannot stop what you're doing and choose happiness like it's some sort of cafeteria food. There are many underlying factors to our feelings. It takes time to develop the mindset to be a happy person.

Happiness is really more complex than you may think because it deals directly with our physiology. There are four main chemicals in our brain that influence our happiness in some way. These chemicals are hormones known as dopamine, oxytocin, serotonin, and endorphins. We don't need to get into the specifics of these chemicals, but just know that certain experiences and activities can help to release these hormones, significantly affecting your state of mind. For example, exercising will help release endorphins, which will affect your happiness and give you the strength to power through your workout. The more you exercise, the more endorphins are released, and the more energy you will have to keep moving. Have you noticed that when you're happy, you have more energy than when you're sad? There is definitely a physiological component to this. If you are feeling down, try doing something physical like walking or even jogging in place. The bottom line, when you create happiness for yourself, there is a particular chemical response. This chemical response creates more feelings of happiness, which, in turn, creates more of these chemicals inside of us. We can certainly say that happiness begets more happiness, so if you have the opportunity to create happiness in yourself, do so, and this will result in a positive domino effect.

Think about your recent history, and remember those times you were truly happy for whatever reason. How did you feel? Well, how did you feel besides being happy? Did you have more energy? Were you more willing to get out and do things? Were you more willing to meet people? Happiness can do a lot to increase your quality of life and your overall well-being. You see the world differently and are more willing to see the good in other people. For lack of a better expression, happiness can bring more joy into our lives. No wonder it is an emotion people go after.

Anger

This is simply unavoidable. All of us become angry at some point in our lives. We do not all express our anger in the same manner. Some people are explosive and let the world know how they feel. Other people are quiet and stew in their anger until they either get over it, or it builds up so much that it boils over. Anger is a normal emotion to have based on various situations and circumstances. Unlike happiness, it is not an emotion most of us strive for. Most people do not wake up and intentionally seek out ways to make themselves angry. Unless they get some strange excitement from it. There are many people who are drama queens who will purposefully find ways to anger themselves, just so they have something to complain about. We are not here to talk about these people. For the rest of us, it is something we like to avoid. However, at any moment, something can occur that will anger us, and we can't stop ourselves from feeling this way.

Even though we all express anger in different ways, it is generally characterized by feelings of hostility, frustration, resentment, and bitterness, among other things. Even if a person is the silent, angry type, their facial expressions, and body language may easily give away their mood. People who let their anger get out of control will often behave in aggressive manners and even resort to violence. Excessive anger has even lead to self-destructive behavior like drinking, hurting one's self or having angry outbursts at some of the worst times. This is definitely an emotion you want to keep under control, or else severe consequences will come your way.

Anger has also been associated with negative physical health consequences. The physiology of anger can be quite complicated, however, in simple terms, the first sparks of anger can activate certain centers in our brains, resulting in the cyclic release of various hormones throughout the body. These hormones create various physiological responses like increased heart rate and blood pressure and can also reduce digestion because blood is diverted away from the gut and to the extremities. The body can begin experiencing a fight or flight response, which means they are ready to run from danger or face it head-on. These various hormones also reduce the effectiveness of our immune systems. Therefore, prolonged and uncontrolled anger may lead to an increase in illness and even chronic diseases. Anger that is ignored for too long has been associated with various cardiovascular diseases, diabetes, and even cancer. It is not okay to be a chronically angry person both for your mood and your overall health.

With all of the problems that anger causes, it seems to be an emotion that has no value. This is not true, though. As we mentioned before, anger can release hormones that create a fight or flight response, which is essential for getting out of dangerous situations. It is not as easy to fight and protect yourself when you are happy. Anger can also allow a person to express their feelings and dislike for something, opening the lines of communication and making changes happen. Anger can also be useful when a person wants to clarify their needs. When a person dislikes something and it makes them angry, they can use that to motivate them to express their concerns. Anger, even though it is a negative emotion, can still have value as long as it does not get out of hand. There is such a thing as too much optimism. Being too optimistic can put you in bad situations from being too trusting. Having a small amount of anger may help you judge a situation more critically, potentially saving you from harm.

Think about all of the time you have been angry. Did you feel good afterward? Well, it probably depends on the results. If you managed your anger well and used it for beneficial purposes, then you probably didn't feel too bad. However, if you became angry and this caused you to have an outburst or made you do something you regret, you probably felt awful. While anger is a common emotion and often cannot be stopped, what we do with the anger matters tremendously. If you're on the road and another driver angers you, don't act on that anger. Take some deep breaths and allow yourself to think everything through. If need be, you can even get off the road for a few minutes when you have the first opportunity. Whatever you need to do to avoid a drastic situation, do it. In the end, you will feel much better than if you acted negatively on your anger.

The funny thing about anger is that it is not always caused by someone else. It can be something you did yourself. For example, if you stub your toe on a table, the feeling is not very pleasant. It can actually feel like one of the worst pains you have ever had. This pain leads to anger. Some people will be able to calm down by taking a deep breath. Other people will lose their minds and kick the table, hurting their legs in the process, leading to more pain and anger. Which path would you rather choose?

Sadness

Sadness is another emotion people often have as a result of either outside circumstances or a person's own thoughts. Sometimes, if a person has negative thoughts about something, whatever it may be, it can lead to sadness. Also, sadness is a result of many of life's circumstances, like the death of a loved one, losing something of value, dealing with a chronic illness, ending a relationship, or having someone close to you go through difficult times. There are many things in life that can make us sad and when they do, we go through feelings of hopelessness, grief, disinterest and decreased mood. These feelings are usually short-lived, but prolonged sadness may lead to depression or other mood disorders. These mood disorders can have severe end results if not addressed properly.

Unfortunately, when people experience sadness, they often engage in behaviors that can lead them to a worse position they were already in, effectively increasing their sadness. People who are sad will not take a healthy approach in many instances. Instead of talking about their emotions, people will suppress them, and isolate themselves. Also, they may do things like self-medicate, drink excessively, or engage in other destructive behaviors. The level of sadness a person experiences will usually be the result of the root cause. For example, losing a loved one will cause more distress than missing a dinner date. Everyone feels sad once in a while; however, prolonged sadness can severely depress your mental health, ability to function, and be productive and also impact your relationships. While sadness is not necessarily depression, it can create many of the same after-effects mentally and physically.

Just like with the other emotions, sadness has a physical component to it. Sadness may also increase stress levels and increase blood pressure. Some studies have suggested a literal "Broken-Heart" syndrome when a person dies from sadness due to a broken heart. Now, this is rare and mostly related to prolonged issues; however, sadness can lead to excessive stress and decreased immune system function, causing a condition known as cardiomyopathy, which is an enlargement of the heart muscle. An enlarged heart muscle will cause our cardiac function to diminish over time.

While sadness is considered another negative emotion, it can certainly create some good in our lives. First of all, sadness actually improves your memory. This is true. Several studies have shown that people had better recollection of events when their mood was low. They seemed to be more focused and aware of what was going on when they were sad. Whereas, someone who has happy was less focused and paid less attention to details. People in a state of sadness also appear to have better judgment, especially as it relates to people. They are able to provide more critical assessments than when they are happy. People who are in a happy state are more likely to misjudge something or someone for good when, in reality, the opposite is true. This is essentially false optimism.

Finally, a negative mood, like sadness, will increase a person's motivation. People will be more likely to push through and move forward when in a negative state of mind, unlike happiness, where people will be more content and unmotivated. It makes sense that people will increase their drive because they want to get out of their current state of sadness. Of course, this is contingent on their sadness being under control. Excessive sadness will lead a person to be sedentary. If a person is happy, they will less likely want to change their current circumstances, so their motivation decreases.

Transient sadness is not a bad thing and may even help you move up in life. Never be ashamed of being sad either, because it is a normal emotion to go through. If you need to reach out to somebody, then do it. Chronic sadness will eventually lead to severe mood and physical disorders. If this negative emotion is prolonged, then you may need to get professional help. Don't let people tell you to get over it. This will happen in your own time.

Fear

Fear is an intense emotion that is the result of perceived danger, whether real or not. When a person senses that they may be in an unsafe situation, they go into survival mode, and their fight or flight response kicks in. During this time, our heart rate rises, our muscles become tense, our digestion slows down, and we become more alert. Fear is a major defense mechanism for us. It puts us in a state of mind that prepares us to handle whatever situation we may be going through. For example, when we are walking down a dark alley, we begin to perceive possible danger based on not knowing what is around us. We are on a much more heightened alert because we feel an imminent threat. Our body is now ready to respond to anything that may impact our safety. We will be ready to run or fight, depending on what happens. All of this is because of our fear. Even though we don't like to feel afraid, it is a necessary emotion to have for these types of situations. It may save our life at some point. The firefighter who was able to run into a burning building, the mom who was able to lift the immovable object off of her child, the lady that was able to outrun her attacker, and the hiker who was able to fight off a wild animal, were all going through the fight or flight response, resulting from fear.

Many people live their lives purposefully with a sense of fear, as this allows them to always be more alert, focused, and driven. These are certainly positive elements of fear. Fear is an emotion we all have, and it is absolutely essential during many moments in life. Take this as a precaution though. Just like with anger, certain physiological processes occur in our bodies when we are in a state of fear. Prolonged and uncontrolled fear can also lead to many mental health and physical health consequences. Also, there is a term known as paralyzed with fear. In this case, a person is completely controlled by fear rather than having control over it. This leads to a person physically unable to react to danger.

While fear is an emotion that is a response to an imminent threat, there is also the issue of anxiety. Anxiety is more related to anticipated threats or what could go wrong. This can be something like being fearful of giving a speech later or worrying about how you will do on a test. While it may not give the same heightened response as fear, it can still give us some similar reactions, just in a milder form. A small amount of anxiety keeps us alert, focused, and sharp. Too much anxiety can cause us to freeze up. Just like all other emotions, it needs to be balanced.

Disgust

Disgust is an emotion we experience when we find something revolting. This may be physical disgust or moral disgust related to reprehensible behaviors. Physical disgust can be triggered by things like bad food, bad smells, the sight of blood or other gory scenes, and death. Moral disgust can be triggered by things like watching someone lie, steal, or witnessing any number of immoral acts. Disgust is one of the major emotions we carry and it is believed to have developed so that the body has a way of protecting itself again something harmful, like food or toxins.

Here are a couple of examples of physical and moral disgust. When you take a bite of food and realize the ingredients used may have expired based on the taste, you immediately spit out the food. This is an example of physical disgust. When you witness someone bullying a person weaker than them, this will create a sense of moral disgust as you despise the bullying behavior. You may even go over and intervene.

Surprise

We all love a good surprise, don't we? Well, it really depends on what the surprise is. A Surprise is a really quick response to something completely unexpected. An unexpected party of some sort is definitely a welcomed surprise. An unwelcomed surprised would be someone jumping from behind a tree and scaring you. Whatever the case, a surprise is being startled by something unexpected. Just like with fear and anger, it will trigger a fight or flight response momentarily. Depending on what the surprise is, it can help to get out of a threatening situation. If someone jumps out from behind a wall and attacks you, your fight or flight response will kick in and help you fight the person off or run for your life.

As we can see, emotions do not just affect our mind and mood, but also our physical health in ways we cannot even imagine. They all serve a different purpose and have different triggers. We experience these, and various other moods throughout the day, and this greatly affects our mental function and physical health. Our mindset and physiology are constantly changing with these changes in emotions we are going through. We have to be consciously aware of allowing our emotions getting out of control. Otherwise, it will negatively impact our emotional states, mental health, physical health, and relationships.

Our bodies react to what we feed them. So, if you are allowing your body to get out of control with anger, for example, then you will more likely lose control every time you become angry. However, if you learn to control and manage your anger, it will become a habit over time. We are creatures of habit, and if we continuously keep our emotions well managed, it will become natural for us.

We used this chapter to thoroughly explain what emotions are and how different emotions affect us. In the next chapter, we will be discussing how we can use the various emotions we have to our advantage. Managing our emotions is crucial in order to live a well-balanced life full of success.

Chapter 2: What is Emotional Intelligence?

Think back during your school years and remember all of the subjects you were learning. They were probably teaching you math, writing, science, and all of the subjects that would bring you the knowledge and increase your IQ. As you got older and went through high school and college, you probably started learning subjects geared towards a particular career path. However, did they place much of an emphasis on your emotional state? Did they teach you about controlling your thoughts and feelings? Did they show you how to manage your emotions in order to use them in a productive manner? Did they express the importance of emotional intelligence? If they didn't, this is quite mind-boggling, as many people who have reached adulthood will tell you just how valuable it is. It may be one of, if not the most, valuable skills you will need. The sooner in life, you start learning them, the better. Of course, don't feel that it is too late to start learning today.

We are not saying that what you learned in school is not important or valuable. It absolutely is and may even be essential to your job function. However, what matters the most is not your IQ or level of intelligence per se, but how well you are able to manage your emotions, even in the direst of situations. For example, a paramedic can have all of the knowledge about emergency medicine in the world. If they are not able to stay cool, calm, and collected in the field, their knowledge becomes futile. A pilot must learn to stay calm and focused, even when everything around them is going wrong. This is where having a high level of emotional intelligence comes into play.

What exactly is emotional intelligence? It basically has the ability to manage and guide our emotions, as well as other peoples' emotions. It is being able to distinguish between different emotions we have, use emotions to guide our behavior, and also adjust emotions according to the environment we are in. We discussed a varying number of emotions, as well as the positive and negative consequences they can have. The negative consequences that can arise from different emotional states reinforce just how important it is to not let them get out of hand. This is what emotional intelligence is all about. When we have a high level of emotional intelligence, we are able to influence our everchanging emotional states in a manner that is controlled and provides us great benefit. At a moment's notice, we can go from a state of happiness to extreme anger. If we don't understand how to control this emotional shift, we may act in ways that will create major problems. If you are walking down the street and are in a pretty decent mood when suddenly a car drives by and splashes water all over you, how would you react? Think honestly about this, because your answer reflects your emotional intelligence. Remember, we are asking how you would REACT, and not how you would FEEL.

Emotional intelligence also has to do with managing the emotions of other people. Of course, we cannot control what other people think. This is definitely not a book about mind control. What this means is being able to use other peoples' emotions for the benefit of everyone, including yourself. If someone is angry with you, they may criticize you in many ways. You may be able to use this criticism to learn more about yourself and the other person. Also, if a person is angry, you may be able to use this to help motivate them to make positive changes. This is what a person with emotional intelligence would do. On the other hand, a person who lacks this skill will simply get angry at someone who criticizes them and will dismiss them entirely.

Emotional intelligence is an absolutely essential skill to possess in order to gain success in any area of your life. We say that emotional intelligence is more important than the intelligence quotient because it is not just about what you know; it is how you use it. You will not be able to use what you know properly if you are not in a state of mind to think about it properly. Even if you don't know that much about a particular situation, when you have your emotions under control, you will be able to think clearly and critically about it, and still find some answers. On the other hand, if you know how to handle a situation, but you are an emotional wreck, everything will fall apart. For this reason, your state of mind is more important than what you have in your mind.

Let's go back to the example of the paramedic from earlier. This emergency responder has all of the knowledge in the world about CPR, critical medicines, driving an ambulance, and handling just about any emergency situation that comes up. However, when he arrives on the scene, he is overzealous, angry at times, and becomes paralyzed with fear. Suddenly, all of that knowledge that we spoke of is practically nonexistent. Even though he knows the theory of what he is supposed to do, he cannot use it in this situation, because he does not have his emotions under control.

There is a saying that there are people who do, and those who don't do, teach. We are not in any way trying to insult teachers here. Teaching is a very noble profession, and people who enter this profession deserve our respect. This statement simply helps to illustrate that some people have all of the knowledge, but may not be able to utilize it in a real-world setting. They do not have practical application skills to be able to use their knowledge. We learn theory by reading, and we learn to use the theory through practice. This brings us to our next point in the book.

Building Emotional Intelligence

Now that we know how important emotional intelligence is, how do we increase this skill in ourselves. None of us are really with the ability to control our emotions. We learn slowly throughout the years how to manage our emotions and use them for the good of everybody. This takes a lot of practice and experience. As an example, the emotion of fear is often sought out by many people who are thrill-seekers. They purposefully put themselves in uncomfortable situations in the hopes of training their bodies and making it easier for them to handle fearful situations. When a person has been exposed to incidents that bring them a certain level of fear, they learn how to control this emotion properly. When they learn how to control their fear, they will be more alert, focused, and responsive during various life circumstances without letting their fear control them.

Over time, a person who has gone beyond their own comfort zone on a regular basis has more ability to handle new situations in life, because they are more mentally and physically ready. Not only are you molding your mind, but also your body to adapt quickly to changing environments. Have you ever seen a person who lives in a warm climate come to a colder environment? They are probably bundled up from head to toe, while other people around them are wearing a simple long-sleeved shirt or thin jacket. This is because the person is not used to the cold like the people who live there are. Once this person puts themselves in this situation more often, they will slowly adapt to the cold and will likely need fewer layers to put on. This holds true for fear as well. The more situations you put yourself in that have an element of fear to them, the more adaptable you will become because you are used to not being in a comfort zone. When we say an element of fear, this does not mean living your life in fear. This is not a semantics issue. These phrases have a completely different meaning. Living in fear means you avoid risk and play it safe. Living with an element of fear means you live beyond your comfort zone. Do not confuse the two.

Since we can practice controlling the emotion of fear, we can also do the same with other emotions. Many people go through positivity training to help train their minds to think in an optimistic manner. Many people live their lives with a negative mindset, and they train themselves to see the bad in everything. Our emotions produce our thoughts. Our thoughts produce our actions. When you speak of emotional intelligence, we are referring to controlling our thoughts and actions that are a result of something we can't control, which are our emotions. We will now discuss various techniques you can use to enhance emotional intelligence. Use these techniques, and you will be handling your emotions in no time.

Become Self-Aware

The first step in coming up with a solution is recognizing there is a problem. If you can't see the problem, you won't know what to fix. When you have self-awareness, you have the ability to evaluate your emotions, thoughts, strengths, and weaknesses. You are also able to understand how these things affect you and those around you. Being self-aware gives you the ability, to be honest with yourself. If you are not honest with yourself, then you will never know what your positive and negative attributes are. We all have our good and bad qualities and it is nothing to be ashamed of. It is one thing to have confidence in yourself. It is another thing to be narcissistic and has delusions of grandeur. With the same token, there is a difference between critiquing yourself constructively and looking down on yourself. You can be positive while still being realistic, and this is essential to improving your self-awareness.

Not everyone has the ability to be completely honest with themselves. It is hard for them to find their weaknesses for a variety of reasons. In order to increase self-awareness, we can also use the assistance of a friend. We are not talking about your nicest friend who will just tell you what you want to hear. There is a time and a place for that. For this situation, you want to seek out your most honest and critical friend. That friend that will tell you like it is and be 100 percent upfront with you is the best person to help you increase your self-awareness. We will never be able to see ourselves as objectively as other people do. Having a good honest friend who knows you well can help you understand your shortcomings. If you have several honest friends, then that's even better. Take advice from all of them and have them hold you accountable. From here, you can rectify your shortcomings. Or, at least start thinking about them intently. Remember, even if your friends are honest, it is still from their vantage point. They may not always be right. Listen to what they say seriously and assess which areas you can improve in. You can also utilize help from a stranger who won't be worried about hurting your feelings. However, they may not know you well enough to give you constructive criticism. Make sure the feedback you receive is useful and not just insulting. Being more self-aware is the first, and probably the most important step in becoming emotionally intelligent.

In reality, whenever we get criticized, it is our natural instinct to feel attacked. We feel like that person is bashing us and treating us fairly. They do not know our situation and, therefore, have no right to comment on it. This may be true to a certain degree. Criticism may be unfounded and based on assumptions. However, this does not mean there is no kernel of truth in this situation. Instead of taking critiques as a personal attack, we need to look at them objectively and see how we can use them to better ourselves. Even the greatest people in our history have been criticized. In fact, they were probably criticized more than anybody else. The difference is, they used it as fuel and a learning moment. We can all do the same.

Being Motivated

Yes, becoming motivated is part of emotional intelligence. There is an asterisk we need to put here. This does not mean that we are chasing people, money, or careers. This motivation we speak of has to do with a desire within ourselves to succeed in life. We do this for our own pride and self-worth. This makes us feel good about ourselves, and when we feel good about ourselves, we are in much more control of our emotions. If our motivation is solely fueled by the need to obtain wealth or material things, then we will never be truly satisfied. While it is okay to go after a better job or live in a bigger home, things like this cannot be your only motivation for success. If so, you will be going after them for the rest of your lives and never truly be happy. If you create an intrinsic desire to succeed because you want to do well in this world, then you will be in a better mindset.

One of the ways psychologists suggest to increase motivation is to track your own progress on paper. However big or small the progress is, write it down. This progress is your own and does not need to be compared to anyone else. Just make sure you track it. Also, when you reach certain milestones with your goals, reward yourself. But, only reward yourself when you reach the milestone, or it won't mean anything in the end. Motivating yourself is a significant step on the path to creating emotional intelligence.

Self-Regulation

Many people assume because they are full of emotions that they have a high level of emotional intelligence. If this were true, though, all of us would be emotionally intelligent. The purpose of emotional intelligence is understanding and managing our emotions in a productive manner, not how many emotions we have. In order for this to occur, we must self-regulate ourselves. We spoke earlier about being self-aware. That was just the first step in the process. However, self-awareness alone will not fix our problem. You can be self-aware that you are an emotional wreck and then not do anything to fix it. First, we must recognize the problem through self-awareness, and then we must work to solve it. This is where self-regulation comes in. Believe it or not, even though we cannot control the biological responses to the various emotions we feel, we can certainly control the behavior that comes from them. We can self-regulate ourselves to make sure we do not lose control of our emotions and run amuck.

Have you ever heard people say that they weren't responsible for what happened because they lost their temper? They believe that they can't control their emotions and are not responsible for what they do. These people are lying to themselves. They can manage their emotions, and so can you. One of the most effective and science-backed ways to regulate our emotions is to practice mindfulness. We do this by taking in deep breaths when we feel the urge to completely lose control. Before you do something, you will regret, slow down and take some deep breaths. A good 20-30 seconds of deep breathing will help you calm your mind and deal with a situation more coherently. Of course, you may not always have 20 seconds, so just a couple of deep breaths will work in the short term. Even a small amount of conscious breathing can help calm your nerves, clear your head and allow you to think more coherently. When you think more clearly, you can control all of your emotions better and vice-versa. A few seconds of mindful thought can vastly change the results of a situation.

Let's go back to that road rage example from earlier. If someone cuts you off and you get angry, you have two options: 1) Let your anger take over, yell and scream and go after the person. 2) Stop for a couple of seconds and take some deep breaths, think about where you are and the consequences of what you might do, and then let the anger go. With the second option, you will keep driving, and nothing else will come from it. With the first option, someone is either getting hurt or going to jail. If that few extra seconds can prevent harmful injury or loss of freedom, then it is certainly worth it.

We can certainly get way more in-depth into mindfulness with deep breathing exercises and meditation, but that will take up a whole different book. For now, just know that being more mindful will bring more clarity to your thoughts and feelings.

Don't mess up your entire life because you lost control of your emotions.

Empathy

Part of having emotional intelligence is also being able to manage the emotions of other people. For example, if a person is shouting at the top of their lungs, it is not a good idea to shout back at them. This will make the problem worse. Empathy plays a big role in this. Empathy is having the ability to understand the emotional make-up of other people and treating them according to their feelings. The most important thing about showing empathy is finding a balance. Many people become emotionally numb after being around so many emotional people for so long. They grow tired and lose interest in feeling for anyone. On the other hand, people feel so much for others that it is all they think about. They never want to do anything to disrupt anyone's emotional state, and this is not possible either. People in this situation are often the ones who end up becoming numb. They cared too much until they did not care at all. It is important to not let this happen. In order to have emotional intelligence, we must have the ability to manage the emotions of others while also taking care of ourselves. Learn to keep this balance throughout life. It is tricky to say how this can be done; however, you know yourself better than anyone else. If it gets to the point where you feel you are giving in too much, then it may be time to pull back a little. Remember that you must take care of yourself while taking care of others. Also, never allow someone to guilt-trip you. They are using your own emotions to have power over you and this is unacceptable.

Social Skills

Good social skills are created from an amalgamation of the first four dimensions of emotional intelligence that we spoke of. When we develop self-awareness, motivation, self-regulation, and balanced empathy, we have all of the makings of someone who is emotionally intelligent. An emotionally intelligent person has the ability to manage people and their needs, can control their own emotions without going crazy, is able to inspire people, and is genuinely a happier person. All of this mixed together improves a person's social skills too. The more you socialize, the more you will continue to understand yourself and others, and the more emotionally intelligent you will become.

What is a common trait about people that are popular and well-liked among their peers? They are easy to approach, are kind and generous to others, work well with people, aim to inspire and not put down, and just have an aura about them that makes them very likable. Increase your emotional intelligence, and you will also be well-liked by those around you.

Be Around Like-Minded People

While this is not necessarily a step in becoming emotionally intelligent, it can certainly help us form the habit. Be around, like-minded people. Basically, what this means is surround yourself with people who are emotionally intelligent. This is not always possible because we encounter so many people in our lives. However, just do the best you can. When you are around people who know how to handle their emotions, you can inherently learn to do so yourself. If you are around people who are completely disorganized with their emotions, you may pick up some of their traits too. The bottom line is, surround yourself with emotionally intelligent people to learn how you can become one also.

With all of the advantages that being emotionally intelligent gives you, it is no wonder that having this skill significantly increases a person's success rate in every area of their lives. It is also clear that it is significantly more important than IQ, because without it, what you know will mean nothing because you can't use it. We will get into the specifics about how emotional intelligence is a necessity in all areas of your life. For now, we will talk about how to tell if a person has emotional intelligence.

Signs Of Emotional Intelligence

Many experts, including a number of psychologists, agree that having a high level of emotional intelligence greatly increases our chances of success. Psychologist Daniel Goldman was one of the first to bring to prominence the ability to manage our emotions and how it plays a major role in the success of our lives. The idea has taken off ever since and has influenced many people in how they think about emotions and their relationship to success.

It is undeniable how important being in control of our emotions truly is. In this section, we will discuss some of the ways to tell if we have healthy levels of emotional intelligence for ourselves and others.

1. You are able to think about feelings. Being emotionally intelligent means you have the ability to recognize emotions in yourself and others. You have the ability to assess the emotions, their root cause, how you can use them to your advantage, and just how the particular emotion is making you feel at that moment. If you can think about feelings in real-time, then it suggests you have a high level of emotional intelligence. If you have ever been unaware of why you are feeling a certain way, having the ability to perform this crucial step will help you change all of that.

2. You have the ability to pause and reflect on the moment at hand. Essentially, you stop to think before you act or speak. This is a true sign of having emotional intelligence. There are many people among us, even the most influential, who spit fire their words and just say the first thing that comes to mind. The words go from their brain to their mouths with no filter. Many people also act on impulse, rather than taking a moment to think about what they're doing. This can lead to many embarrassing moments and even making commitments that they cannot fulfill. These people do not show signs of high emotional intelligence. Before you speak or act, take a moment to pause and think about what you are about to do. This can save you immensely from saying something hurtful, doing something you regret, or committing to something you cannot fulfill. Have you ever said something instantaneously that you wish you could take back? Well, you can't go back and fix the past, but you can certainly learn from it. If you follow this step, you can prevent this from happening in the future. Imagine how much pain and heartache a few extra seconds of thinking can save you.
3. You work hard to control your thoughts. You cannot prevent emotions from entering your mind, but you can control the thoughts they produce. At the very least, you can control acting on those thoughts. For example, if someone bumps into you purposefully and does not even

apologize, your immediate reaction will be to get angry. This is normal and not something you can control. However, everything afterward, you can. You may have thoughts of shoving the person down. You can stop these thoughts and then go on your way. A person who is in control of their emotions will do just this. However, a person who is not in control will continue to have these thoughts, will possibly yell something out, and may even go as far as pushing the person down. This person did not control his thought or actions, and for this reason, lost control. They will now have to face the consequences of losing control.

4. You are authentic in what you do and say. When you say something, you mean it. You don't share anything and everything, but you are comfortable sharing major parts of your life. An emotionally intelligent person is secure in who they are and is comfortable showcasing it for those who need to know.
5. You accept criticism from others and use it as a learning opportunity, rather than being offended. Instead of wondering why people are attacking you, you ask yourself how you can improve, based on the criticism. Even if you learn nothing, at least you get an idea of how other people perceive you. Take in constructive criticism and use it to your advantage. Don't let your feelings get hurt over it. If someone is not providing criticism, but insults, then ignore them. There is no time for that. However, if you

look at many of the criticisms you receive objectively, you may realize the kernels of truth that exist in them and use them to improve yourself and the situation. You may not realize you are quick to anger until somebody tells you. You also may not know you appear sad until someone mentions your body language. Listening to these comments can help you tremendously.

6. You have the ability to show empathy. You connect with others well and take time to understand their situation, rather than jumping to conclusions. Having empathy for someone is a major part of managing their emotions.
7. You praise others for a job well done. Some people are jealous or envious type. When someone else does something well, they make excuses about what advantages a particular person may have had. It is common that a person will shun another person's success, because they feel they did not work for it, oftentimes, not knowing the full story. The truth is, a person with emotional intelligence will have no problem giving people credit for the work they do. They are secure enough to know and not care that praising others will take the spotlight off of them. Some people just can't handle this. They always need to be the center of attention and get praised incessantly. When you praise others, you are not just showcasing your emotional maturity, but also inspiring the other person to be the best they can be. People love getting praised for what they do, so be the one

to do it when it is warranted. Do you find yourself getting sick to your stomach when other people are getting praised and not you? Well, you may need to change your mindset here. Giving someone praise does not bring you down a notch; it simply helps raise the other person up. You don't have to build them a pedestal. A simple thank you goes a long way.

8. You have no problem admitting when you are wrong and will apologize when you are. Of course, apologizing does not need to be done only when you're wrong. It can also help to smooth out a situation. Usually, when something does go wrong, there are multiple reasons why, and they do not all fall on one person. Being willing to apologize not only shows emotional intelligence, but also humility. This will draw people to you. Apologizing does not make you weak. In fact, it is a true sign of strength. Apologize, and then move on. You will continue to grow.
9. You are willing to forgive and forget. We have heard this a lot. When you hold onto a grudge, you are hurting yourself more than the other person. This is very true. Imagine if someone handed you a bag of garbage. You can either get rid of it or hold on to it. If you hold on, it only affects you, and not the person who originally handed it to you. When you forgive and forget, you release the pressure on you and free your emotions from being held, hostage. You get rid of that garbage bag. This shows extreme maturity and emotional intelligence.

10. Going back to criticism, not only are you willing to receive constructive criticism, but you also give constructive criticism. People don't enjoy getting negative comments about them, so it is important to reframe it in a way that you still get your point across and it is helpful. Here are some examples related to a person stocking the shelves: "You are doing it all wrong! what are you thinking? Let me show you!" These comments are negative and show hostility. They will not be received well. Here is another way of putting it: "Thank you so much for stocking the shelves. I appreciate it. You're doing a good job, but let me show you how we prefer to stock these items so you know better for next time." This second example gets the point you need across, and also is not hostile. The person will likely be more receptive to it.
11. When you make a commitment, you keep it. This goes for a small commitment as well as a large one. It may not seem like canceling dinner plans is that big of a deal, but remember that there's another person involved. They took time out of their lives for these plans too, and simply not showing up without a good reason, or overlooking the plan, is very disrespectful to them and emotionally immature on your part. Whether it's a small commitment like a dinner plan or a large commitment like a business meeting, show up when you are supposed to and keep your word. Remember the part about taking a moment to pause? This is very valuable at this moment. Pause before

you make a commitment to make sure you actually can make it. It will save you from having to cancel it later. When you do, fulfill that commitment. A person with emotional intelligence keeps their word.

12. A person with a high level of emotional intelligence is willing to help others. When you help other people, it positively impacts their emotions too. Helping others will help you too.

These are just some of the signs of emotional intelligence. If you see these qualities in a person or yourself, know that you are dealing with someone who is truly in control of their thoughts and feelings. If you do not possess these qualities yet, don't worry, you still can. It will take discipline, but you can start building your emotional intelligence, no matter what stage you are at in life. In addition, this will be a lifelong learning process. A person may never develop all of these traits perfectly, but they will be able to improve themselves for the rest of their lives.

We are all humans. The chances of us being in control of our emotions at all times for the rest of our lives is quite impossible. It is quite a daunting task to ask of anybody, no matter how emotionally intelligent they are. However, it is imperative that we control our emotions in the most critical moments in our lives. A surgeon cannot lose control in the middle of an operation, but they can go home later that night and cry their eyes out.

Emotional Agility

We want to use this section to mention emotional agility because it is an important concept that ties in with emotional intelligence. Emotional agility is the ability to be flexible with one's emotions and use them in a way that is most beneficial to themselves. When we speak of this subject, we are referring to the ability to stop and think about our emotions, recognize them, and then respond in a way that is appropriate for us and is also in our best interest. This also is a reference back to pausing before acting on your feelings. There is a space between the stimulus that triggers an emotion and the actual response to that emotion. In that space lies our power to choose our appropriate response. This moment in space may be brief, but it can make a world of difference if we practice being emotionally agile, rather than just reactive. This space is truly a powerful moment.

The phrase emotional agility was coined by renowned psychologist, Dr. Susan David, Ph.D. She believes that our ability to recognize our emotions and react accordingly based on our values will help us to bring about the best in ourselves. When we remain emotionally agile, we maintain the ability to cope with the various challenges around us. Let's look at an example. "Mike loves his job and wants to be as productive as possible. However, all of his new coworkers are lazy and uninspired. This causes Mike to eventually give up and stop trying. He simply does not care because his coworkers are lazy. Mike is not practicing emotional agility here. He is allowing his emotion of anger and/or frustration to take control of him. This is causing him to go against his values of hard work and productiveness. If Mike took a moment to assess his emotions, he would realize that other people's work ethic has no bearing on his own. Also, he may be able to come up with ways to help inspire his coworkers, so they become more productive. Having emotional agility helps us tremendously in navigating the world we live in and responding appropriately in various circumstances.

We hope that you have enjoyed this chapter on emotional intelligence. Our goal was to provide concrete explanations about the importance of emotional intelligence and how it is one of the most necessary skills to have to succeed in this world. No matter what path in life you are going down, having the ability to assess and manage emotions in real-time is a true art form and one that will bring you much prosperity. We will now describe how this valuable skill is needed in every facet of our lives.

Chapter 3: Being Emotional at Work

We will now be getting into specifics about how emotional intelligence is a necessity in our everyday lives. Regarding work, this can refer to working for a company or working as an independent business person. We will touch on both and how important it is to have emotional intelligence at work or when running a business. Either way, it is a necessity to keep your emotions in check and not allow them to get out of control, no matter what emotion it is. Our work and livelihoods depend on making sure cooler heads prevail. Think about this anytime you feel like losing it on somebody at work. It will not be worth the aggravation.

There is no way around it. Most of us need to work or provide some way to bring in income. Unless you are one of those people who never have to worry about money ever again, you must learn about maintaining emotional intelligence in the workplace. If you are one of these people, well, there is more you can learn in further chapters, so please keep reading. The truth is that you will be making a variety of decisions while at work, and you will also have many outside forces that will bring out many of your emotions. These outside forces include your boss, coworkers, workstation, workload, office atmosphere, the temperature, and even what they may be serving in the cafeteria. In the workplace, there will be many factors beyond your control that will trigger the various emotions that exist within you. Certain environments may put you on a heightened response in general due to the nature of the work. While some of these negative emotions will make you want to lash out, it is certainly not a path you want to go down.

If you do not practice emotional intelligence at work, then you will be faced with severe consequences, including being shunned by your coworkers, getting reprimanded by your boss, creating a toxic work environment, and even losing your job. Many of us dream of walking into our boss's office and telling them off. Unfortunately, doing so will be more detrimental to you, then to your boss. It may feel good at that moment, but it will guarantee you a first-class ticket out of that organization. Giving someone a piece of your mind is certainly not worth losing your livelihood over. There are much more productive and diplomatic ways of handling a situation.

Imagine that an employee becomes so infuriated with their boss, that they march into their office and tell them off using some of the most colorful languages they can think of. This employee completely lost control of their emotions, and will now have to deal with the repercussions, which will most likely be him losing his job. If he’s lucky, the boss may cut them some slack, especially if they have always been a good employee up to that point. However, that black mark will always exist on his record and he can never take it back. The boss will probably not be so forgiving the second time, so it is best to just avoid it happening the first time.

If this employee practiced some emotional agility, he could have taken a moment to assess the situation, recognize his emotions, calm himself down, and then think of a better approach to handle the situation. By doing this, he could have walked into his boss's office in a calm manner and expressed his concerns with a level head. He may have been able to provide some solutions to various problems himself. His boss would have probably appreciated that as well. It would show that the employee cares about the company and is proactive. The outcomes of this second scenario will be much better. Unfortunately, the first scenario occurred, which created a major rift between the two that may never heal. If you are at work and feel like your about to explode, take a deep breath, and also step outside if you can. Bite your lip at that moment and prevent yourself from doing something you will regret. Yelling and screaming at your boss will bring you joy for a moment, but controlling your emotions will bring you joy in the long run.

Furthermore, when dealing specifically with coworkers, your nerves may be tested on a regular basis. With all of the different personalities present in an office environment, dealing with a multitude of emotions within yourself and others will be inevitable. Your coworkers may even try to rile you up on purpose, either because they're jealous or they get some sort of pleasure out of it. Don't let this happen. Practicing the different dimensions of emotional intelligence (Self-awareness, motivation, self-regulation, empathy, and social skills) is of utmost importance. You may not like your coworkers; however, you will have to have a working relationship with them. The last thing you want to do is create a toxic and uncomfortable work environment. For this reason, increasing your emotional intelligence is essential. It will be beneficial for you and those whom you work with.

The most important thing to know is that no matter what emotion you are going through at the present time, allow yourself to analyze everything before responding, whether it's with words or actions. To reiterate, no matter what emotion you are going through, take the time to assess before taking action. While happiness is a positive emotion, there can be some negative things to come out of it. We spoke earlier about how sadness may cause a person to be more critical, aware, and focused. Happiness, on the other hand, may cause a person to be less focused and attentive to details. For this reason, the person may commit to certain things without fully understanding what's going on. A person who is going through a happy state will more likely take on extra work, extra shifts, extra responsibilities, and extra commitments in general, without even knowing if they can handle them or not. This can create a major problem down the line because if you commit to something and then back out of it, it will make you look bad. Think before you respond. Doing so will showcase a great amount of emotional intelligence.

When you are more emotionally intelligent in the workplace, it will improve your outcomes, improve your ability to communicate, improve your decision-making skills, improve your relationships, and just make you a more likable person. This will not go unnoticed. Eventually, when a higher position opens up, or more money opportunities exist, you will be in line to get these opportunities. This will all be because you know how to manage emotions in your workplace. Higher emotional intelligence equals higher success in the workplace.

You cannot control what happens to you, but you can control how you react to it. If something or someone upsets you, it is a natural response to become angry. You may not be able to stop the anger, but you can keep it from controlling you. This is absolutely essential in the workforce. Other people's toxicity does not have to be your toxicity. Think about all of the disaster movies you have seen. We will use the pilot landing a damaged plane as an example. During this period, everyone is shouting, freaking out, and losing control. People are even passing out from fear. The only people who are not losing their minds are the ones who are successfully helping to land the plane. In the movies, this is often depicted as one of the pilots and someone in air-traffic control. These people are not only successful at managing their emotions but also managing other peoples' emotions. At the very least, they are able to ignore the noises around them and stay focused on the task at hand. Even in the movies, they know the importance of emotional intelligence at work.

Since we spoke about controlling our emotions in a workplace setting, we will now discuss the importance of it as a business person or entrepreneur. If you run the type of business that has employees, then you will still have to deal with various personalities. As the business owner, the onus is on you to create a positive work environment. In order to do this, you will have to practice the steps of becoming emotionally intelligent. You can know the business inside and out. You can create a budget without even thinking about it. You may be an expert marketer. Having all of these attributes is great. One thing is for sure though, none of it will matter if you cannot manage your emotions and those of the people around you.

Once again, practicing the different dimensions of emotional intelligence is crucial. As a business owner, your productivity, output, and success all depend on it.

1. Be self-aware so that you know yourself, know what you can handle, and understand your emotions.
2. Motivate yourself so that you can be your best self and improve every day. Your employees deserve this, and so do you.

3. Self-regulate yourself so that you manage your emotions properly. This will be tough, knowing that it is your business on the line, and you will have the most to lose.
4. Be empathetic towards your employees. Your employees will have different needs and possess different values. It is important for you to be understanding of this in order to create a productive work environment.
5. While you may not be at work to socialize, having decent social skills will allow you to connect well with your employees. Your employees deserve to be communicated properly.

If you run a sole proprietorship or an independent business of some sort that does not have employees, then you can bypass some of the emotional intelligence needs as it relates to employees. However, keep in mind that no matter what type of business you run, you will likely have clients and customers to answer to. They all deserve your very best. They get this by you having emotional intelligence. As a business owner, you will have to make many decisions that will affect yourself, and other people, so you need to keep your emotions in check and your mind calm. Leave your ego at the door and do what is best for you, your business, and your clients.

As a business owner, you will have a variety of emotions running through your mind. There will be many highs and lows. Success in business is never a straight line. There will be many dips and valleys, so you will need to control your excitement when your business is doing well and manage your sadness, anger, and frustration when your business is down. Many businesses fail within the first couple of years. A lot of this has to do with people not being able to control their emotions. They make poor judgment decisions when the business is successful and can even become lazy. Furthermore, they will often quit and walk away when things are down, instead of pushing through. While short-term sadness and anger can motivate a person to work through tough times, allowing these emotions to go, haywire will result in major mood disorders that will become difficult to manage. When you can no longer manage your mood, you can no longer manage your business.

No matter what type of environment you work in, managing your emotions is critical to your success. Having emotional intelligence will not only benefit you but also the place of business in general. Many of the top professionals in any field will have a high level of emotional intelligence. These include business people, actors, athletes, and artists. It is nearly impossible to reach that level without it. Imagine being the CEO of a major corporation. You are expected to make some very important decisions that will affect hundreds of people and their families. If you decide poorly, the consequences can be detrimental. The CEO must be focused, and not be swayed easily by their own emotions. Also, they cannot let the thoughts and feelings of other people cloud their judgment. It is important for the CEO to manage the emotions of the employees as well and put himself in their shoes to a certain degree. Through all of this, the CEO must make crucial decisions with a calm mind. A CEO who has their emotions regulated will be able to make sound decisions most of the time and do it with confidence. They will not be right 100% of the time, but they will be able to continue making major decisions because they have the mindset to do so.

Let's go back to the story of the paramedic from earlier. In the original story, the paramedic had all of the knowledge in the world but did not have the mindset to use it. By the time he arrived at the emergency situation, he was so confused about all of the emotions going through his mind, that he fell apart at the seams. Now let's imagine him being a newer paramedic. He has much of the basic knowledge he needs for the job but just is not very experienced. He is, however, a very calm person who knows how to keep his emotions balanced. When he arrives on the scene of a medical emergency, he is able to process his thoughts and feelings and remain calm even under the direst circumstances. For this reason, he is able to use his basic knowledge while on the field and then have the patient transported in the ambulance to the nearest hospital. The patient was transported safely, and the original scene was cleared up.

Because this young paramedic was able to control his emotions, he remained calm and was able to manage the situation with relative ease. Even though he did not have as much knowledge as the original paramedic, his state of mind allowed him to use what he knew productively. This story showcases how emotional intelligence is superior to knowledge and IQ. We are not suggesting that knowledge is not important. It absolutely is. However, if you are not able to utilize the knowledge, because you can't keep a calm head, then it becomes futile in the end. Learn the information you need to do the job, and then develop the mindset you need to do it.

Do you practice emotional intelligence in the workplace? If you have a job, then you probably do. If you didn't, chances are you would not last long in your position. You probably already possess some of the skills needed for emotional intelligence at work. Now, you just have to increase it. There is always room for improvement.

Chapter 4: Being Emotional With Goals

We all have goals that we strive for, whether they are long-term or short-term goals. These goals require a lot of time, dedication, persistence, and hard work. There will be times that are so hard that you just want to quit. However, if you do, you will lose everything you worked for. When going after your goals, whatever they may be, it is important to realize the peaks and valleys that will exist. Things will never go up in a straight line. Many people set their goals based on what they see in other people. They see someone who is successful in their chosen field and want to become like them. What they fail to realize is that successful people did not just end up where they are by chance. They worked up to that point and had many falls along the way.

With these up times and downtimes, you will also have a varying number of emotions to contend with. You will be happy and excited during the great times, and be sad and angry during the low times. The important thing is to always stay focused on your end goals. In order to do so, you must have control over your emotions at all times. So before you start setting major goals in your life, start increasing your emotional intelligence. Also, understand that other people have, and continue to go through the same successes and failures that you will. If they can do it, so can you.

We will use an example of setting a longterm goal. Imagine being a college student and wanting to apply to medical school after finishing your undergraduate degree. Your ultimate goal is to become a doctor. As you approach the end of your sophomore year, you realize that you will need more science classes, so you register for them the following semester. Also, because you are behind, you decide to take a summer class also. You have good grades and are confident they will get you into a good medical school. However, your dream is to get into one of the top five medical schools in the country, so you work harder.

During your junior year, you begin taking your advanced level science classes, but they are quite difficult. You persist through hard work and focus and manage pretty decent grades. You also need to take the medical college acceptance test. You feel overwhelmed and are having a hard time balancing everything. You take control of your emotions and continue studying for the exam. When you take it, you do not do as well as you would have liked. Likey not well enough to get you into a top-five medical school. You continue to work hard through your senior year, hoping that your grades and extra-curricular activities will make the difference. When it is time to apply, you send out applications to multiple schools, including all of the top five medical schools on your list. After this, the waiting process starts. The anticipation is hard to bear, but you continue to remain focused, knowing you still have to graduate.

Several months go by, and you begin receiving replies to the various applications you sent. To your surprise, and dismay, all of the ones you received so far are rejection letters. This puts you in an extreme state of sadness. After all of the effort you put in, you got rejected by the majority of schools you applied to. Including all of the top five colleges. For several days, you feel like doing nothing. The rejection letters really devastated you. You feel like giving up because you may not be good enough. After a few days, you realize that you are wasting your time. You cannot change what happened, so you look towards the future. There are still a couple of schools you have not heard from. If you get into one of those, you can still become a doctor. After this, you get yourself together and become focused again on your longterm goal.

Several more days go by, and you get another letter in the mail. This time, it is from a local medical school, and they inform you that you have been accepted! This excites you tremendously as you realize all of the hard work paid off. You do not let this excitement distract you, though. You know that hard work is just beginning. Nonetheless, you obtained your goal of getting into medical school and are well on your way to becoming a doctor. After four years of medical school and a lot of trials and tribulations, you finish medical and are now a doctor ready to start residency. You have made it!

In this scenario, you had a longterm goal that you were able to meet, despite various challenges along the way. How were you able to get through these challenges? By working hard, remaining focused, and, most importantly, managing your emotions properly. Whether you were happy or sad, you did not waiver from your end goal, because you did not let your emotions take control over you. There were times that you were close, but you did not let it happen.

As we can see, when going after a goal, particularly a longterm goal, there will be successes and failures along the way. However, if you want to reach that goal, you have to keep moving. This means that no matter what emotional state you are going through, you have to maintain your focus and keep your emotions in check. Short-term goals will have similar moments, but there may not be as many peaks and valley along the way because of the shorter time period. This does not mean that you won't be experiencing a variety of emotions during the process. Whatever your goals may be, large or small, make sure to build and maintain your emotional intelligence. Otherwise, your goals will be dead before you even start.

In general, write down your goals and assess them regularly. Determine if they are what you really want and then work hard to get them. A strong work ethic, determination, focus, and emotional intelligence are what you need to obtain your major goals in life.

Here is a breakdown of how the different dimensions of emotional intelligence apply to goal-setting.

- Be self-aware, so you understand your emotions and know if you are stable enough to get to your desired goal. Whatever the goal may be, there is the potential for many highs and lows. Understanding this upfront is a huge step.
- Be motivated so you will have the internal desire to succeed and move closer to your end goal every day. Even if it's a short distance, progress is still progress. Whatever you do to move closer to your goals every day, write it down. This will help to keep you motivated.
- Self-regulate yourself so that your emotions are under your control. As you pursue your goals, you will be on an emotional ride like nothing else. Don't allow this to distract you. Keep your emotions regulated, and you will keep your goals in focus. When you become happy with major accomplishments, be joyful, but be humble too. Don't let the excitement overtake you. Otherwise, you will become complacent at the moment when you need to keep your momentum going. If you become angry or sad during the low points, then use these emotions to help push your through until everything is performing well again. Don't allow the anger or sadness to control you.
- Empathize with others, but do not give up too much of yourself. People will need your help along the way, and you can manage other peoples' emotions for the

betterment of them and yourself. Remember though, that keeping up with your goals will require you to still be focused, and you cannot do this if you are constantly giving in to other people. As an example, when going after a particular goal, you may run into people with various personalities. You will have to be able to manage their behaviors because you will need them to get to the next level. However, do not allow yourself to completely give in to their feelings and lose yourself in the process. Empathize with other peoples' emotions, but maintain a balance with your own.

- You will have to talk to people along the way, especially if your goal requires dealing with other people. When you have the previous four dimensions down, your social skills will improve dramatically, allowing you to pursue your goals in a stronger fashion and with good social skills.

When we mention goals here, we are referring to professional goals, like finding a new job, starting a business, writing a book, or learning a new trade, etc., and also personal goals like exercise and relationships. You will have good times and bad times for both. Whatever your goals are, take them very seriously.

Chapter 5: Being Emotional at Home

Emotional intelligence does not just have to do with success in the business world. It also deals with success at home. Even at home, your emotions will fluctuate continuously throughout the day, causing you to be on an emotional roller coaster. In order to keep your house in order, your family unit strong, your relationships intact, and maintain your sanity all at the same time, you must have a high level of emotional intelligence. Many people are able to maintain their composure at work, but then they fall apart when they get home. This can result in catastrophes in their home setting, and it is certainly not fair to people in our personal lives. We will break this chapter down into different areas of someone's personal life and discuss how emotional intelligence is crucial in each one.

Emotional Intelligence and Personal Relationships

For this section, we will be referring to friends and relationships outside of the home. We will detail emotional intelligence and immediate family in the next section regarding your home. We all have a multitude of personal relationships throughout our lives. These can include friends, neighbors, distant relatives, romantic partners, and clergy, etc. We generally want our personal relationships to be healthy and fun. Just like in any other setting, when you are dealing with a variety of people, you are dealing with a number of different personalities, and many of them will clash with each other, even with yours.

While we may have a harder time keeping our emotions regulated with our personal relationships, it is still imperative that we do. Allowing our emotions to get out of control may damage our mental health, physical health, and relationships without us even realizing it. Many of our close friends or family may be bringing their negative mindsets into our lives constantly. Many people tend to give free passes to people who bring toxicity in their lives if they have known the people for a long time. We are here to tell you that this must stop in order for you to become emotionally intelligent.

If you have people in your life who are constantly testing your emotional sanity, then these relationships may need to change. We are not saying you have to eliminate these people from your life, per se, but what we are suggesting is that you must still learn to manage yours and other people's emotions for the benefit of everyone around, no matter who you are dealing with.

Some of your most personal relationships may cause you to become angry, frustrated, or sad on numerous occasions. While this may be unintentional in most cases, it still needs to be addressed. You cannot allow people to simply create a variety of emotions in you without having some type of control over them.

Furthermore, it is still good to practice empathy in these moments. Being empathetic will allow you to understand a person and their feelings better. Certainly, take an empathetic approach before doing anything else. Remember though, to still maintain balance. Even though you are dealing with a good friend, do not allow them to use you completely. Do not allow yourself to become fully empathetic to them to the point you stop taking care of yourself.

Once you have utilized all of the steps in gaining emotional intelligence, then it is time to assess your situation in life in regards to your personal relationships. In these moments, you will have much more clarity and be able to determine what paths you want to take. Do you want to get closer to some people? Do you want to cut ties with others in order to bring more positivity to your life? We cannot give you the answers, but we are confident that you will be able to find them yourself, once you are able to think more clearly and with less emotional baggage.

You certainly do not want to lose close relationships with people because you could not keep your emotions under control. Whenever you are dealing with someone you are close to, always remember to practice emotional agility, as this will allow you to respond appropriately to other peoples' words and actions.

Our actions can have longterm, and even permanent damage. Remember this when thinking about your personal relationships with people. There is a great analogy to use here of a boy putting pins on a wall. A young boy was once always yelling at people and hurting their feelings. One day, his dad had enough of it. He told his son that each time he hurts someone's feelings, to push a pin into a certain section of a wall. The young boy started doing this for almost a week. At this point, the dad had him stop. He then told his son to go say sorry to all of the people he hurt, and each time he does, pull one of the pins out. After a couple of days, all of the pins are gone. The dad then points to the wall and informs him of the pinholes. The son is confused until the dad tells him that these holes represent the damage that occurs when hurting someone's feelings. Saying sorry may take away the words, but they won't take away the pain that went with them. Words and actions carry a lot of weight to them. If you are about to react to an emotion, think about the damage you may do.

Emotional Intelligence and Your Home

Home is meant to be your resting place. It is your castle and the place you are meant to feel safe. It is also a place where your family or those living with you are meant to feel safe. For this reason, it is highly important to maintain a high level of emotional intelligence. In order to keep your home in order, you must also keep your emotions in order. If not, your home life will be severely disrupted, and this is not fair to you, or anyone that may live with you. It may seem easy to maintain your emotions in your own home. However, many people do not realize the number of triggers they may have that will set them off.

Some of these triggers include major repairs, bills, household chores, safety issues, and family drama. Yes, even though our homes are meant to be our safe place, we will still be surrounded by many factors that can set us off and disrupt our emotions. Being able to manage a home and family, while also taking care of yourself, will require a high level of emotional intelligence. Unfortunately, many people, including children, grow up in a toxic environment due to their home lives. They have to deal with negativity, drama, and even abuse constantly, and the main reason for this is because people do not know how to handle their emotions. If you are feeling overwhelmed, just realize that you can solve all of your problems if you just keep your emotions in check and clearly think your way through to the solutions. Remaining calm will bring much more value than losing control. Losing control will simply disrupt your home environment.

The last thing you want to do is create chaos in your own home. The place where you are meant to live, rest, and be at peace should remain this way. It will be beneficial for you and those who surround you. Being in a constant state of emotional upheaval is not the type of environment you want to live in or raise a family in. Have you ever walked into a home and felt the vibe right away, whether they are positive or negative? People feel the same vibes in your home as well, so be conscious of this.

Emotional Intelligence and The Public

By the public, we are basically referring to anyone outside of your home that you don't really have any type of relationship with. This can be a random guy at a grocery store, the person in the car next to you, or the lady behind the movie ticket counter. In your personal life, if there was ever a time to make sure you have your emotions are in your full control, it is when you are dealing with the general public. You will be around a number of different people who are doing their own thing and trying to mix with other people the best they can. With all of the distractions combined with the fast-paced world we live in, everyone seems to be in a heightened state. This causes emotions to flare up at random times, and we never really know what will set someone off. The world can become a crazy place in an instant and it is extremely important that you buildup your emotional intelligence in order to deal with the society that exists out there.

As you integrate yourself into the general public, you will be faced with a multitude of situations that will trigger every emotion you have at some point. Here is a simple scenario. When you walk out of your front door in the morning, you may receive a package that is a gift from a friend. This will make you excited. As you get into your car and start driving, you may get cut-off by someone, and this will cause you to become angry. When you arrive at the store, someone bumps into you without saying sorry. This will make you angry again. When you up to the counter to pay, you realize the person in front of you paid for your groceries. This makes you excited and grateful. As your driving to your next destination, you receive a phone call, and the person on the other line informs you that a friend is in the hospital. This makes you sad and worried. You decide to make a detour to the hospital. When you arrive, you go to the information desk and the people are not very helpful and even dismissive. This will make you frustrated because you want to see your friend. When you finally find out what room he is in, You go and see him. You are sad for him at first, but then you realize he will be okay, and this once again makes you happy. As you walk out the door, the staff gives you a friendly goodbye and this makes you even happier.

During this period, there were many emotions you went through. These are not counting the ones you had just walking around without any major triggers. There were also many opportunities for you to lose control of yourself and make a major scene. Luckily you didn't, so your day did not turn out too poorly. If, at any point, you lost control over your emotions, your day could have been vastly different. You may have never gotten to the grocery store, you may never have been able to see your friend, and you may have never gotten back home. When dealing with the public, we will be around many different people and situations, and any number of them can cause us to lose control. For this reason, having emotional intelligence is very important for our everyday living.

The vast majority of the population has already been practicing emotional intelligence while living amongst society. If they had not been, there would be many more out of control incidents being reported. There are many instances where people are just unaware of what is going on. They are in their own world constantly and barely realize what is going on around them. People drive erratically without realizing it. People will stand in the middle of an isle way, blocking traffic from both directions. People bump into others without even apologizing. People are constantly on their phones, completely ignoring the world around them. There are plenty of opportunities for people to lose their cool in public. Luckily, they have enough control over their emotions to at least control themselves from making a scene.

Emotional Intelligence and Personal Thoughts

Even when you are sitting home alone with your own personal thoughts, it is still important to have a high level of emotional intelligence. How you think, how you believe, and how you perceive yourself plays a major role in how you will act in the future. We must still control our thoughts in a productive manner in this situation; otherwise, we will be unfocused, lost and unmotivated. Even when you are sitting alone, you are still making decisions for yourself. One of the hardest battles people fight is with their own thoughts. This is because they allow their own emotions to control them. This can be for a variety of reasons. A person may be sitting at home and still be angry about something that happened to him a couple of months ago. While they are sitting alone and stewing over it, their anger is controlling them completely and clouding their judgment. Some of the best decisions a person can make are when they are in a quiet space with some time to think. Unfortunately, if a person does not have control over their emotions, they will still make poor decisions.

The good news is, when you are sitting home alone, you have more time to get your emotions in check. You have more time to get into a state of mindfulness, which will allow you to balance your emotions and regulate them appropriately. Use these quiet moments you have at home to your advantage. Use the time wisely to work on exercises like meditation and deep breathing, which can help to calm your nerves, help you manage your emotions, and allow you to think more clearly. If you still allow your various emotions to run rampantly through your mind, this will not only affect you at the moment but for a long time afterward until you decide to take control of your thoughts and feelings.

Even when you are sitting home alone, how you think, how you act, and how you respond is still important. Be mindful of emotional intelligence, even when you are by yourself. How you think is what you become. Become someone exceptional. Don't allow negative emotions to create constant negative thoughts in your mind.

Emotional intelligence is important in every aspect of our personal lives. Whether we are dealing with ourselves or other people, we have to remain in control of our emotions. If we don't, we will damage our relationships, thought-processes, and ability to function. We may even ruin our lives or someone else's. Unfortunately, not a great emphasis has been put on the value of emotional intelligence. However, it is one of the most critical skills to possess in order to lead a successful life in every way. Fortunately, there are many real-life opportunities to develop this skill, so use them whenever you can. In your spare time, study and develop the different dimensions of emotional intelligence. You will be glad you did.

Chapter 6: Emotional Intelligence and Our Health

We discussed in chapter one about the various physiological responses different emotions have on us. If we don't keep our emotions in check, it can lead to severe health consequences in the future. We will get more in-depth about this here. In this chapter, we will discuss how much of an impact controlling our emotions will have on our physical and emotional health. Every emotion, every thought, and every response or action has a domino effect as far as the various body functions that are triggered. While we are all different in our physiology, the general way that our bodies function is the same. In most cases, positive emotions will create a cascade of positive responses within our mind and body. On the other hand, negative emotions will have the opposite effect.

Happiness

Happiness is widely considered a positive emotion, and something people strive for. For good reason too. Being happy puts you in a good state of mind and promotes a wealth of health benefits. For starters, being happy encourages many healthy lifestyle habits. When we are happy, we are more likely to eat healthy foods, exercise or be physically active and also get the proper amount of sleep. So when you are happy, you actively pursue being healthy because you want to.

Furthermore, happiness can boost your immunity. When we are in a chronic state of being happy, we can actually help prevent serious illnesses, because our immune systems are more adept to fight them off. The science is still not completely understood behind this. However, the various glands and hormones that are activated with this particular mood may play a major part in boosting our immunity. Many research studies have shown various participants to be at a lower risk of developing a cold or chest infection when they were happy, while those who were less happy, were at a higher risk.

People may not realize it, but when they are in a constant state of stress, they are slowly killing themselves. While stress is certainly normal under certain circumstances, if it is continuous, it can carry a higher risk of heart disease, poor sleep, diabetes, and high blood pressure. These health issues are related to a hormone called cortisol, which is released during times of stress. When we are happy, we are less stressed, and this effectively decreases our cortisol levels. The combination of changes to our physiology, coupled with more healthy behaviors, makes happiness into an emotion that we must strive for to improve our heart health and overall well-being. Of course, we do have to take all of this with a grain of salt. Although many studies have shown the link that happiness has to good health, the science is certainly not set. Whatever the case, being happy makes us feel good, so it is certainly a good emotion to have.

There does not seem to be any direct links between happiness and poor health. All of the studies suggest that happiness is good for your physical and mental health, and the more you strive to be happy, the better you will be. The only time happiness can really go overboard is if it makes you unmotivated and uninspired. Meaning, you become complacent and no longer go after major goals. Furthermore, extreme happiness can lead to unchecked optimism, which can create a false sense of security. This can lead people to believe they are invincible and take unnecessary risks. Hiking Mount Everest with guides and proper training is a reasonable risk. Hiking Mount Everest alone and with no preparation is a dangerous and unnecessary risk. Don't become so happy that you become foolish. Beyond this, happiness is great for our health and our life. This emotion is not always easy to obtain. In fact, at times, it may seem impossible. But happiness is attainable, so do your best to strive for things that make you happy. Happiness occurs when you create a life for yourself that you are proud to be a part of.

Anger and Other Negative Emotions

We will discuss the health effects of anger and other negative emotions here because many of our physiological responses are the same. While many of the negative emotions, like fear, anger, and sadness, are necessary at certain times of our lives, we cannot deny their negative health consequences either. Unlike happiness, these negative emotions increase our stress level, creating major hormone imbalances and depleting the chemicals in the brain required for happiness to occur. The more stress we experience in our lives, the fewer chances we have of becoming happy again. Therefore, chronic stress can actually decrease our lifespan!

When we allow our negative emotions to get out of control, we create a cascade of responses that result in poor health outcomes in the long run. These can include major issues with heart disease, including coronary artery disease, heart attack, and stroke. With the increased stress levels, you have an increased level of blood glucose also, which can become difficult for your body to manage. Excess glucose is taken up by our cells for energy; too much extra glucose will remain in the bloodstream. For a short-term period, it may not be a big deal. However, if it continues for the longterm, the blood glucose levels can eventually lead to diabetes. Certainly, many other factors will play a role like lifestyle choices, diet, and genetics, but stress is definitely a major contributing factor. Heart disease and diabetes will eventually impact other organ systems in the body, which will impact our overall health in a negative way.

Unlike with happiness, the hormones involved with stress actually decrease our immunity. This will put us at greater risk for various illnesses and chronic diseases. Our immune system is like our own personal army that will attack and kill anything that it perceives as a threat. If our personal army cannot defend us, then we become prey to many foreign pathogens that can attack and destroy our cells, tissues, and organs. Even getting a simple cut, or catching a common cold can have much more devastating effects. Negative emotions can damage our immune systems, leading to severe health consequences.

In cases of anger and fear, our fight or flight response can be activated. This is definitely an important physiological response that works as a defense mechanism. One of the things that happen at this time is our blood is shunted to our extremities, so that we have the ability to run, hide, and fight if needed. As a result, blood is shunted away from our gut, and this will effectively decrease our digestion for the moment. This is certainly a necessity during times of great stress; if this continues for the longterm, then it will create further health problems. Digestive health is oftentimes overlooked. It is an important factor, though, for our overall well-being. If we are in a state of constant stress, it will impact our digestion tremendously. Poor digestion will cause us to feel bloated, tired, and sluggish, which will lead to further negative emotions like sadness. Furthermore, extended issues with digestion may lead to problems with the heart, kidneys, brain, and other vital organs. People take for granted just how much proper digestion impacts their mood in a positive way.

Finally, dealing with negative emotions for the longterm can lead to mood disorders like depression and anxiety. All of us experience limited depression and anxiety at some point in our lives, but having to deal with these disorders day after day is a whole other story. What is worse, being in a state of depression will continue to make you release various hormones that will further your symptoms. Major mood disorders can also lead to more physical illness, and physical illness can lead to more mood disorders. It is a vicious cycle that will be hard to get out of once you're there.

When you are dealing with negative emotions, in general, you are less likely to take care of yourself too. This includes physically and mentally. You are less likely to eat right, be physically active, sleep well, and do the things you enjoy. The longer you deal with these negative emotions, the worse it will become. Much to the disbelief of many people, these thoughts and feelings are not something someone can just get over. It takes time, effort, and energy. With the building evidence suggesting the link between emotions and health, many psychologists, researchers, and medical professionals are coming together to better understand the connections that may exist.

With all of the major health consequences that come with uncontrolled emotions, it is imperative to gain emotional intelligence. It not only puts you in a better state of mind but can also save your health and your life. After going through all of the challenges a lack of emotional intelligence creates, we can certainly see that this is not hyperbole.

Chapter 7: Every Day Living With Emotions

We have discussed in detail what emotions are and how we must keep them in our control at every moment. Emotional intelligence affects every facet of our lives, as we illustrated in the previous chapters. Now, we will bring everything together by providing hypothetical situations of how having emotional intelligence and the mindset to manage our emotions can completely alter the outcome of many different circumstances. We will provide various stories from the side of having emotional intelligence, and lacking emotional intelligence, in order to showcase how much of a difference the ability to handle our emotions is.

Frank's Mall Story

We will first take a look at a story from Frank at the mall during Christmas time. In this scenario, Frank does not use emotional intelligence, and he pays the price for it. So do many other people.

Frank is headed to the mall a few days before Christmas. He has to do some last-minute Christmas shopping. He knows the mall will be packed, so he is trying to get an early start. Unfortunately, the traffic is horrific on this day in just about every direction. What should have been a 20-minute drive takes over 45 minutes. Frank is pretty frustrated after this, but he keeps his cool for now. Until it takes him another 10 minutes to find a parking space. There are no spaces that are open and when a car does leave, the spot fills up almost immediately. Frank is getting more irritated by now. He just wants to go in and get his shopping done.

As Frank is going down one of the aisles, he sees a person get in their car and turn around. He stops, puts on his blinker, and waits to pull in. He is expecting the car to pull out soon, but he is waiting for what seems like an eternity. Frank begins smacking his steering wheel with his fingers and when the person still doesn't come out after several minutes, he begins blasting his horn. He does it twice and then waits a few more seconds. After this, he blasts his horn again. Many of the people walking around, stop to stare, but Frank does not care. He just wants to park already. Finally, the car comes out, and Frank pulls in quickly. The roads are a bit icy, so the car slips and slides a little bit.

Frank quickly gets out of his car and starts running towards the wall, slipping a couple of times himself on the way there. When he gets inside the mall, there is a huge crown everywhere. He just wants to get to the stores he needs to go and then get out. He finds the sporting goods store, the toy store, the jewelry store, and the appliance store. He only takes about 10 minutes in each store to shop, but it takes over 30 minutes due to the lines. This angers Frank even more, and he begins to really lose his patience. His last stop was the appliance store and the line is moving so slow that he gets out after 15 minutes, puts the blender he picked up somewhere on a random shelf and then storms out of the store.

As Frank is walking around, he becomes a total scrooge as everything starts to anger him. Even seeing Santa on his sleigh makes him shake his head. Frank continues to walk towards the exit as multiple people are bumping into him. He takes it at first until he has a head-on collision with another shopper. Before the guy even has a chance to respond, Frank throws all of his bags on the floor, and then grabs the other guy's shopping bags and throws them on the floor too. Frank then proceeds to give the guy an ultimate tongue-lashing. The other guy starts yelling back, causing everyone around to stop and stare at the insanity. After a few minutes, security comes along and escorts Frank away. All of the witnesses in the area informed security that he was the aggressor in the situation. Which he certainly was.

Frank was still stewing in his rage; when he started to look around, he realized what just happened. He became very embarrassed and did not want to be seen. Not only will Frank not be getting the items he came to buy, but he also ruined another person's day. Actually, he may have ruined many peoples' day because of what they had to witness. All of this occurred because

Frank could not keep his emotions managed properly. Many things did happen to Frank that were beyond his control. However, he definitely could have controlled how he reacted in these various situations.

We will now look at Frank's story from the aspect of him showing emotional intelligence. The outcomes, in many ways, will be different.

Frank leaves his home to go to the mall for some last minutes shopping. It is just a few days before Christmas, so he knows the traffic will be horrendous. He anticipates being in his car for a while, so he made sure to download some of his favorite music. During the drive, the traffic is bumper to bumper and what would generally be a 20-minute drive, ends up being just over 45 minutes. Frank was able to listen to good music the whole time, so he did not mind that much. He did get a little frustrated that it took him so long to find a parking space. Every time one opened up, it would get filled right away.

Finally, when Frank saw someone get in their car as he was driving down the same lane, he stopped and put on his blinker. After waiting a couple of minutes, the car still had not moved. Frank was growing irritated. He did not want to lose that spot, but also did not want to wait forever. He took a deep breath, waited a couple more seconds, and then started driving. As he turned a corner, another car was backing out, so he was able to pull in right behind them. He pulled in slowly as there was a lot of ice on the road.

After parking, Frank got out of his car and began walking to the mall. He slipped a couple of times because of the ice, but then started walking very carefully. Once he got inside the mall, he saw the barrage of people all over the place. He knew it was going to be a very long day. Before he went shopping, he decided to stop at the food court and pick up various snacks that he could munch on throughout the day. This was a smart idea as all of the stores he went into had ridiculously long lines. Even though it took him only 10 minutes to shop in each store, he stood in line for at least 30 minutes in four different stores. He was able to finish all of his snacks, so at least he was not hungry. Frank was tired from all of the shopping, but luckily he got it done.

As Frank walked around the mall, he looked around at all of the decorations and was excited to spend Christmas with his wife and kid. He also had to dodge people so he would not run into them. It was quite chaotic inside the mall with the hundreds and maybe even thousands of shoppers. Frank was definitely ready to get out. Shortly before he reached the exit, he had a head-on collision with another shopper. They both looked at each other for a few seconds. Frank got a little riled up and wanted to tell the guy to watch where he was going, but then took a deep breath. He simply said, “Sorry, excuse me,” and they were both on their way. Frank took a moment to stand against the wall to calm his nerves before making that final dash towards the exit.

After leaving the mall, Frank went to his car and put the gifts away. After sitting down in his car, he drove off to get back home. He was able to get everything he needed from the mall and was happy to be returning back home. The drive home still had some traffic, but luckily, he was able to beat the afternoon rush, so it only took him about 30 minutes to get home.

In the second scenario, Frank was able to showcase his emotional intelligence. By doing so, he was able to avoid a lot of bad situations. He also maintained his mental clarity and was able to get everything he needed to be accomplished. Finally, he was able to get home, rather than be in the custody of mall security for who knows how long. Overall, it was a good day for Frank because he was able to control his emotions. Nothing was different about the day, except for Frank's attitude.

Mary's Story

Mary is a nurse at a local hospital. On one of her morning shifts, there is much more traffic than usual during her drive, and this causes her to barely make it work on time. When Mary arrives at work and receives her assignment, she begins getting a report on her patients. The reports take a while and Mary just wants to get her morning started. After finishing up the shift report, one of Mary's coworkers informs her that they are trading assignments. Mary was upset by this and informed her she already got a report on the patients, and she is not starting over again. She then moved the other nurse out of the way and kept walking. This prompted a meeting with the manager.

The manager informed Mary that her behavior was unacceptable, and she has to find better ways of communicating. Mary hesitantly agreed and then received her shift report on her new patients. She was not behind an hour and had to pick up speed to keep moving. In the meantime, she was receiving a number of calls from the doctors, patients were demanding her attention and her coworkers kept getting in her way. She was on her last nerve and did not know how she would make it through the day. She skipped her lunch and just had a protein bar because she was so far behind. The morning really overwhelmed her and she was ready to end the day. Unfortunately, it was not even halfway over.

Later in the day, Mary was passing out her mid-day medications. One of the patients asked her for some water. Mary said she would get it soon. The patient demanded it right away, prompting Mary to shout out, "You will get it when I am able to get it for you!" The patient was stunned, and Mary walked out of the room. She then passed the remainder of her medications. When she was done, she got caught up on the rest of the charting from the morning. She was still quite behind. When her coworker who traded assignments with her in the morning asked for help, Mary ignored her and kept walking. She left her coworker stunned.

"You messed me up this morning, then tattled on me, and now you want m help?" Mary shouted at her. "Not going to happen." After this, Mary kept walking to get more of her work done. She brought the patient that requested water and left it on his table without saying a word. Mary was nearing the last couple of hours of her day and she was called suddenly into her manager's office. Her manager informed Mary that she had received a lot of complaints about her that day, both from patients and her coworkers about her attitude. Mary did not really know what to say. She knew she lost her cool a couple of times during the day, so there was nothing to defend. She could not really use the pissed off excuse. Her manager informed Mary that she was writing her up for the day.

Mary left her manager's office in an even more foul mood than when she walked in. She just wanted to end her day and go home. She was down to her last hour and spent much of it avoiding people, even some of her patients. When her workday finally ended, Mary went home and laid in her bed. She had no interest in eating dinner or anything else. She just wanted her day to end already.

Unfortunately, there were many things that happened on this day that was beyond Mary's control. However, due to her inability to control her emotions, she made things much worse for herself. There were many parts of the day that Mary could have managed better, resulting in better outcomes for the rest of her shift. She is just lucky no one was harmed and she did not get fired. If she has another day like this, that could definitely become a reality.

We will now look at Mary's day from the perspective of her having emotional intelligence. This will result in many major changes throughout the day.

Mary is driving to work early in the morning. She is a nurse at a local hospital. On this particular day, there is much more traffic than normal. When Mary finds out it is due to an accident; she counts her blessings in knowing it was not her in the accident. About 5 minutes earlier, it could have been her. Mary cleared her mind and notified her work that she was running late. When she arrived, she did not have to rush so much because they knew she was on her way. When Mary arrived, she got her assignment. The patients were quite intensive, so it took a while to get her shift report.

Once Mary was done talking with the night staff, she started getting her stuff organized. Suddenly, one of her coworkers came up to her and stated that they were switching assignments.

Apparently, this other nurse had Mary's patient load the day before and wanted to keep it. This frustrated Mary as it would put her behind tremendously. Mary refused to trade her assignment as she already spent all morning getting the information, plus she was behind already due to major traffic. The other nurse insisted, but Mary had to stand her ground. She was not going to be bullied; she was trying not to lose her cool either.

After a couple of minutes of arguing, Mary took a deep breath and stated that she was sorry, but she already completed her morning reports on the patient, and she would be very behind if she traded patients now. She also explained to the other nurse that she, herself, would also be behind if they switched assignments now. Once Mary saw that the other nurse was still frustrated, she suggested they both discuss it with the manager. Mary explained her situation with the manager and she agreed with Mary. The two nurses kept their assignments as is. Mary was a little bit behind due to the arguing, but only about 10 minutes. She was able to make it up by hustling a little extra.

During the morning rounds, Mary was able to assess her patients, hand out their medications, and take care of her patient's needs with a little help from her coworkers. Mary even had time to take her lunch break, which helped her clear her head for the rest of the day. After lunch, Mary went back on the floor and continued working. The afternoon was busy but manageable fo her. She became overwhelmed at times, but because she was able to keep her cool, she made it through. She also knew when to ask for help.

Later in the evening, the nurse that Mary had the argument with needed help with her patient. At first, Mary wanted to ignore her because of all the grief she caused her in the morning. However, Mary stopped for a few seconds to think about it. There was no reason a patient should not get help due to a personal problem. Also, it could have just been a simple miscommunication. Mary went in to help her coworker with what she needed. She also apologized for the morning and explained that she would have been happy to trade assignments if it would have been requested earlier. The other nurse agreed and thanked her for understanding.

Mary finished up her day, and because she was able to keep her emotions in check, she had a good day overall. Even though nothing else may have changed about Mary's situation, the fact that she showed emotional intelligence, even when it was really hard to do so, completely altered the results of her day. Mary was faced with a lot of challenges from hostile staff members, patients needing her attention and getting a late start in the morning. However, her own attitude is what mattered more for making it a great day. Mary's ability to control her emotions meant that she could end her day satisfied.

Jim at the Gym

We will look now at the story of Jim while he is getting a workout in at the gym. Again, we will look at it from the scenario of having emotional intelligence versus not having emotional intelligence.

Jim arrived at the gym in the morning to get in a good workout before work. This was a great gym, but there were only a couple of elliptical machines, which was Jim's main staple that he loved using. His plan was to get on it right away, but they were both preoccupied. He went to stretch out instead for a few minutes. When looked at the machines again, one of the guys was on there just staring at his phone. Jim went and stood by him for a few minutes, but then he decided to lift weights for a while. He figured the guy would be done by then.

After about 20 minutes, Jim came back around, and the same guy was on the elliptical, barely moving and still staring at his phone. Now, Jim was getting irritated because he only had a short time before having to go back to work. He went up to the guy and told him he needed to use the machine. The guy looked back at him and said he would be done in a few minutes. He then proceeded to stare at his phone again while barely using the machine. The person on the other elliptical was working out hard and had only been going to 10 minutes at this point. Jim did not want to disturb them. He told the person again that he needs to get off the machine now. The guy again just looks at him again and turns back around.

After this interaction, Jim had enough and started cursing the guy out. All of the patrons nearby started looking over to see what was happening. Before any staff members could break things up. Jim had pushed the guy off the machines, causing him to fall down. The guy was irate, and after Jim realized what he had done, he was embarrassed. What made it worse was all of the people staring at him. He realized he acted poorly, but could not change it at this point. Before he was able to help the guy up, several staff members stopped him and escorted him out of the gym. They threatened to call the police if he ever returned.

Even though it is irritating that someone is holding up a machine and not actually doing anything on it, it does not give us any reason to lose our tempers. Unfortunately, Jim acted quite poorly in this situation. He showed some patience at first but then lost control when he should not have. As a result, he could have potentially hurt somebody, made a scene in the gym, and also lost his membership. He could even face some legal trouble if the gym or the guy he pushed down want to pursue and legal action. All of this happened because Jim did not like someone hogging the machine that he needed.

We will now look at how this situation could have been handled differently with the use of a little bit of emotional intelligence.

Jim arrived at his local gym that he has been frequenting for years now. He wanted to get a workout in before going to work. This was a great gym, but it only had two elliptical machines, which was a staple of Jim's workout sessions. When he arrived, both machines were occupied. Jim really wanted to use the elliptical, but he decided to stretch for a few minutes first. After this, he looked over and noticed the guy on one o the machines looking down on his phone and barely moving on the machine. Jim was frustrated by this, but instead of making a scene, he simply went to lift some weights.

After about 20 minutes, he noticed a new person on one of the ellipticals, and the guy from earlier was still looking down at his phone and barely using the machine. At this time, Jim went over to speak to the guy. He explained to him that he needed to use the machine and only had a limited time before going to work. The guy looked at Jim confused for a while, but then got off the machine after he said please one more time. After this, Jim was able to get about a 20-minute workout on the elliptical, which is all that he needed. He got in a good, arduous 20 minutes. When he finished working out, he left the gym feeling pretty good and energized for the rest of the day.

Jim was definitely irritated with the guy for taking up the machine while other people needed it. However, he kept calm and asked him politely to come off so he can use it. This resulted in things turning out well for Jim. He did not embarrass himself or get into trouble in any way.

Susan at Work

Susan had a really fun weekend with her friends. She was able to catch up on a lot of sleep and even went out to a few of her favorite restaurants. Also, her son was staying with her this week so she could spend time with him. As a result, she was unusually happy when she arrived to work on Monday morning. She had a definite skip to her step and was able to get her work started right away. About the middle of the day, one of Susan's coworkers asked if she could cover one of her afternoon shifts for her. Susan, without hesitation, told her she would be happy to. A couple of hours later, Susan's boss asked her if she could take on a couple of extra projects this week. Susan told her that she would be happy to.

The rest of the day for Susan went pretty well; she was able to complete all of her tasks and still felt pretty good by the end of the day. As she was about to leave, Susan was approached by another coworker, who asked if she could give her a ride to a few places after work. Susan was happy to do so. After a couple of hours, Susan went home to get dinner started. She was late and almost forgot she had to pick up her son from practice. When they arrived home, there was no time to cook, so they just ordered from a restaurant.

The next morning, Susan had to get started on one of the projects her boss had requested. It was quite intensive and took several hours to complete. This was on top of her regular workload, some of which she had to push back to the next day. Even though she stayed at work an extra hour. This caused her to barely be able to pick up her son again and be home in time to make dinner. She had to make frozen dinner this time. Susan was a single mom, so there was no one to help her at this time. Before going to bed, Susan tried to answer a couple of work emails to get a head start for the next day.

Susan woke up quite tired and barely able to get out of bed on Wednesday. When she arrived at work, she had to take care of the other project her boss had requested for the week. This one was even more intensive than the first one and took her most of the day. She was not able to do any of her leftover work from the day before or her regular workload for this day. She stayed at work another hour on this day trying to catch up, but then she had to leave to pick up her son again and then try to make dinner. She wanted to cook tonight so she would not have to buy food again. Since her son was only with her for a limited time as she had joint custody, she wanted to give all the attention that she could. She was quite exhausted after dinner and had no more energy or time to think about work.

On Thursday morning, Susan was still tired but tried to get started on her work right away. She was quite behind and had a lot of catching up to do. She normally got off work early on Thursdays, so she could have used that extra couple of hours to get more work done. Unfortunately, she forgot that this was also the day she promised to cover for her coworker. She tried to get out of it, but her coworker said she absolutely had to. Susan kept her promise and covered her shift like she said she would. This caused her to not be able to catch up on her work. She also realized she would not be able to pick up her son. Luckily, one of her neighbors could do it for her.

On Friday, Susan got going on her work again, and she was still behind a couple of days ago. She caught up as much as she could but still had so much more to go. Her boss informed her about the reports that she did not complete. Susan tried to explain why, but her attempts were futile. She was reprimanded by her boss and had to work over the weekend to complete what she was behind on. Her weekend plans had to be canceled and she ended up spending all her day Saturday working. What is worse is that her son had to leave after this weekend to go back to his dad's house. Susan was devastated; she could not spend more time with him, plus she was angry at herself for taking on so much extra work without thinking it through.

This was an example of someone's happiness taking control over them and causing them to lose their ability to assess how much they can handle. As we mentioned before, happiness may lead to unchecked optimism, which can cause a person to take on more than they can handle. This is certainly what happened to Susan, and it ended up spoiling her week and weekend. Be careful to stay in your right mind and don't allow yourself to get carried away with happiness. We will not look at the same scenario; however, this time, Susan will practice some emotional intelligence.

Susan had a pretty good weekend with her friends. She was able to catch up on a few things, and also tried out a few new restaurants. Her son was also staying with her this week, and she would be able to spend some quality time with him. She shared joint custody with her son's dad. When Susan arrived at work on Monday, she was quite happy and it showed. The people she worked with noticed she had a skip in her step. She got to her desk and immediately began working on various projects. At about the middle of the day, one of her coworkers asked Susan if she could cover one of her evening shifts that week. She was tempted to say yes; however, she took a moment to think about it and realized it would cut into the time she would spend with her son. Susan had to tell her no, and the coworker was okay with it.

Later in the day, Susan was approached by her boss to work on a couple of extra projects for that week. Susan knew that these extra projects usually took a lot of time, so she asked about the details. After hearing all that was expected, Susan stated she could take one of them in order to still be able to accomplish her other duties. Susan's boss informed her that he trusted her more than anyone else to complete the requested projects, and he would assign some of her other tasks to another employee. Susan was happy about this and also honored by her boss's compliment. She was happy to take on the two extra projects. Her boss cleared for Susan whatever she had to do the next day so she could focus on what he needed her to do.

As Susan was leaving work, she was stopped by another coworker who asked if she could drive her to a few places. Susan looked at the time and decided she had a couple of hours before she needed to pick up her son. After finishing up, Susan picked up her son from his practice and then took him to his favorite restaurant. She decided this would give them more quality time than her cooking all evening. They had a great time.

The next morning, Susan got to work and began working on the projects that she needed. They were quite intensive, just like she thought, so she is glad her boss cleared the rest of her schedule for the day. By the end, she was able to complete the majority of her work but just had a few things leftover. She decided to stay an extra hour and complete the projects fully rather than having to worry about them the next day. She had them on her boss's desk before she left, and he was very impressed. She was able to spend the rest of the evening with her son, and also did some cooking for the next few days.

On Wednesday morning, Susan was ready to start her day again. Her boss asked her again to work on a small project. She looked at what it was and determined it would only take about an hour. She accepted it and was able to complete it by the end of the day. She had some other work remaining, but she could get caught up on that the next day. She would have time this evening to take her son to the park or the mall. Her coworker, who had asked her earlier in the week about covering her for a couple of hours the next day, reached out to her again today. Susan could see that she desperately needed someone to help her. She figured because her son would be at practice the next day for a couple of hours, she would be able to cover her shift. Susan decided to help out her coworker.

On Thursday, Susan was able to get her work done and also cover the shift that her peer needed. She was done just in time o leave to pick up her son. They went home, watched a movie, and then had dinner. Susan was very excited about spending time with her son. This had probably been the most high-quality time she was able to spend with him.

On Friday, Susan went into work again. When she got there, her boss asked her to work on a project that she could take home over the weekend. Susan refused and explained to him calmly that it was her weekend wither son. He understood. He then asked her if she could work on a smaller project and have it done by the end of the day. Susan accepted and began working. As Friday was coming to an end, Susan was getting ready to leave work and spend the weekend with her son. She finished all of her work for the week and was even able to help her boss with a few extra assignments. She was also able to help out her coworker.

In the second scenario, Susan was much more organized and on top of what she needed to do. She was able to fulfill all of her commitments, and whenever she did make a decision, she made sure to assess it first. Even though Susan was exceptionally excited on Monday, she did not let this overtake her and alter her thought-process. Unfortunately, in the first story, Susan's week fell apart. In the second story, things went quite smoothly, and much of it is because she practiced emotional intelligence.

These various hypothetical situations showcase just how imperative it is to have emotional intelligence in every area of our lives. We used various stories from different environments and show-cased different emotions to help us get an overall view of how real-life situations can be affected by our emotional intelligence. We hope that this chapter brought everything together as far as how beneficial and necessary handling our emotions are in every phase of our lives. The sooner we learn emotional intelligence, the better we will be when we enter our adult years. Make a deep introspection into your own life and see where you are with controlling your emotions. Are you someone who loses control easily, or are you able to manage your feelings throughout the day? Be honest with yourself and determine how much emotional intelligence you need to build in your own life. Emotional intelligence does not necessarily mean controlling what happens to you but controlling how you respond to it.

The Decisions We Make

The life we end up living is all about the decisions we make every moment in our lives. We will make good decisions and bad decisions. Some decisions may not be good or bad, but the best we could come up with for a particular situation. These decisions can be small or major and can affect our lives for years to come. As we saw with the scenarios we detailed above, the results that were created were based on the decision-making that was done. Whatever decisions we make, there are more chances of them producing positive results, if we keep a positive mindset and manage our emotions well. Emotional intelligence is the key to having a successful life, strong relationships, and creating a better future. Next time you react to one of your emotions, stop and make sure it is the correct response and decide what to do next.

Conclusion

Thank you for making it through to the end of *Emotional Intelligence: For Living a Better Life, Becoming Successful at work, and Having Happier Relationships. Learn and Improve Your Emotional Agility, Social Skills and Discover Why it Matters More Than IQ*. Let's hope it was informative and able to provide you with all of the tools you need to enhance your emotional intelligence. Through this book, we wanted to provide an in-depth discussion about how the various emotions we go through have both a mental and physical impact on us. Furthermore, we detailed how we can control our emotions by increasing our emotional intelligence. Above all, without having a high level of emotional intelligence, it will be very difficult for anyone to succeed in any area of their lives. Without having the ability to control our emotions, we will be lost, unfocused and unsuccessful. When our emotions take complete control of us, we lose our ability to function properly and will never be able to create a better life.

No matter how much we know or how talented we are, if we are not able to have the proper mindset for the situation, we will fall apart, and our knowledge will become useless. For this reason, emotional intelligence is much more important than a person's IQ. Whether we are at work, in our homes, driving our cars, or spending time with family and friends, we must be able to manage our emotions and the emotions of those around us. If we do not, not only will we damage our relationships, but also our mental and physical health. Our overall goal was to provide a detailed assessment of the vast benefits of increasing our emotional intelligence. In the end, it is not optional but imperative to learn.

The next step is to further understand your own emotions and then utilize the information we provided in this book to help manage them. Use this book to increase your emotional intelligence, and you will increase your chances of success.

Finally, if you found this book useful in any way, a review on Amazon is always appreciated!

9 780645 018578

Printed by Libri Plureos GmbH in Hamburg,
Germany